From this very serene and spiritual town in the heart of Portugal, all photos in this photobook are taken by my lens.

I hope the photos bring you fond memories of your experience there if you have ever visited. And if you haven't yet, I hope they inspire in you the interest to learn more about the story behind this one-of-a-kind place, Fátima.

Marianne Toma

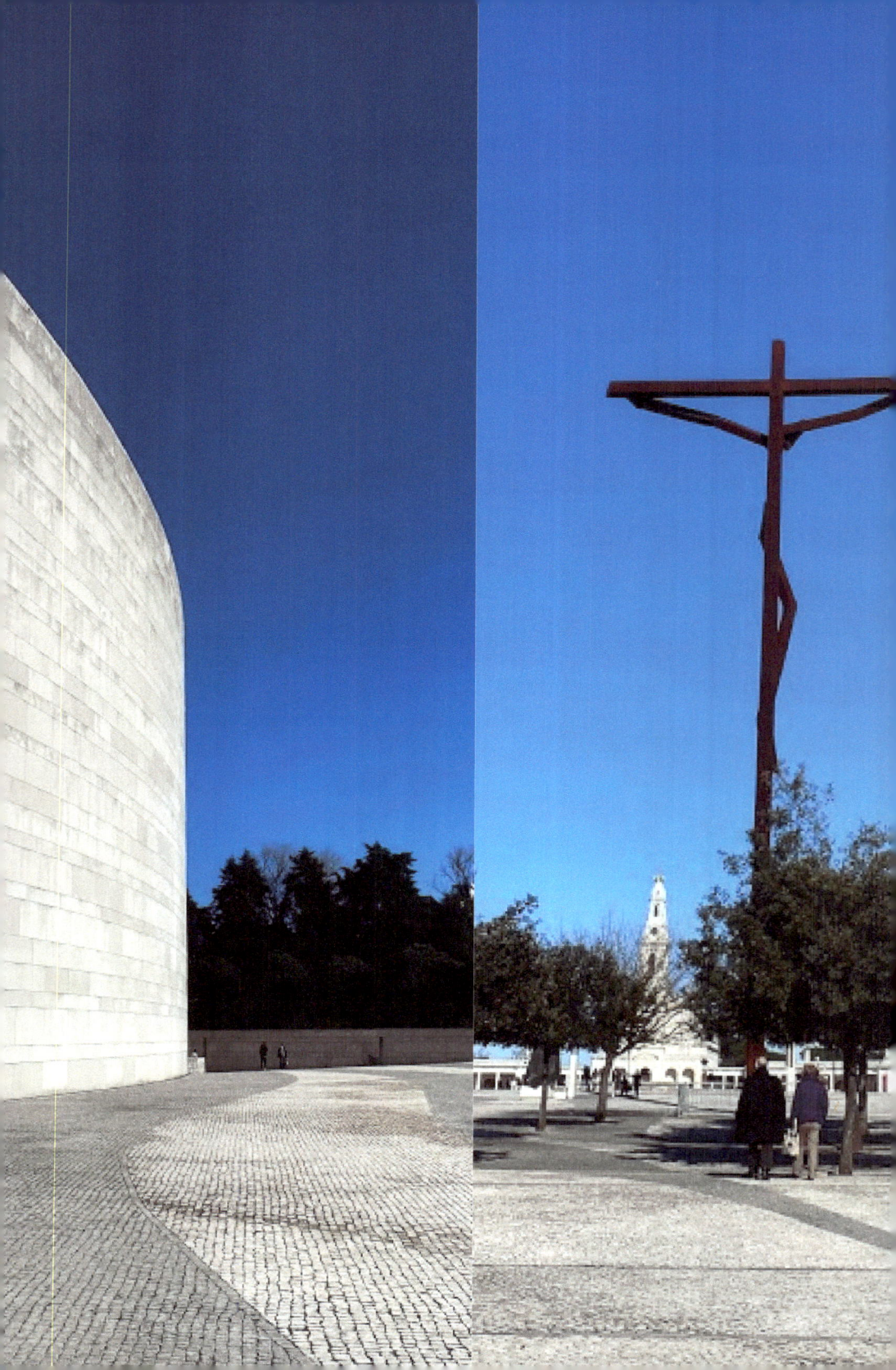

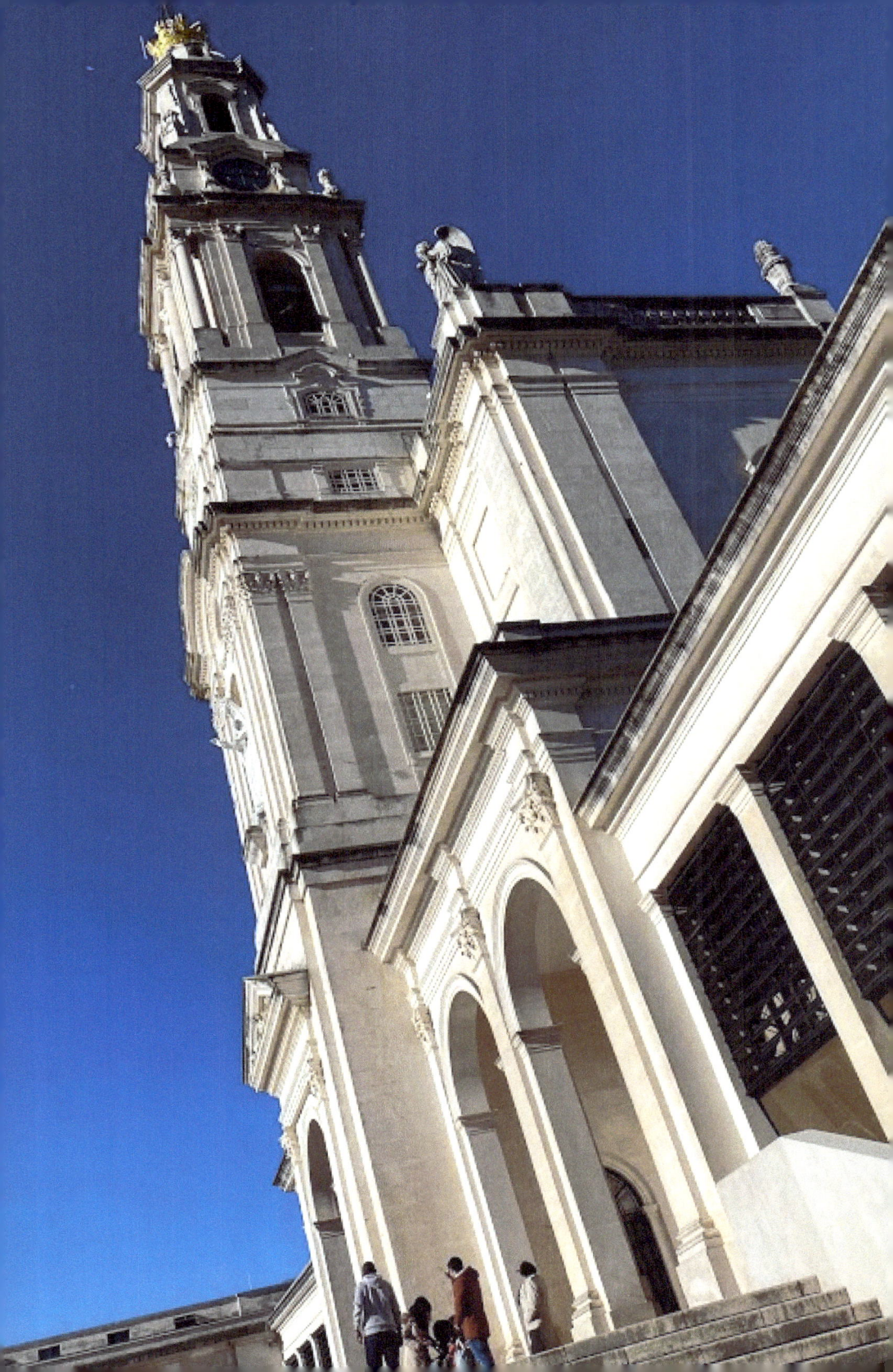

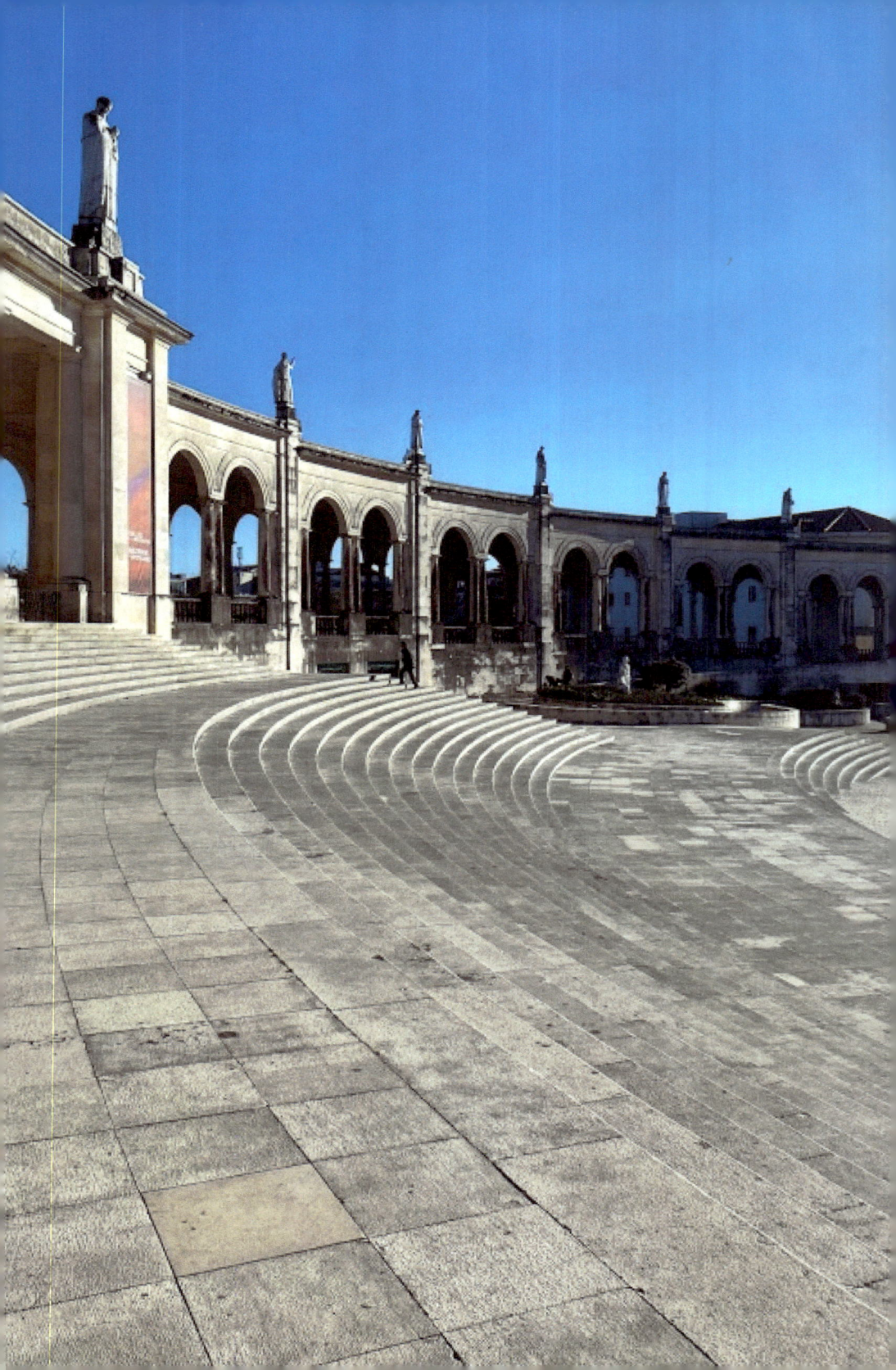

The Origins of Fatima's Shrine

In 1917, during a time of war and uncertainty, three shepherd children—Lucia, Francisco, and Jacinta—reported witnessing apparitions of the Virgin Mary in the small town of Fatima. She delivered to them messages of peace, prayer, and repentance, which would resonate worldwide. The Cova da Iria, where these encounters took place, has since transformed into a sanctuary that welcomes millions of pilgrims annually, each seeking solace, inspiration, or a deep connection to faith.

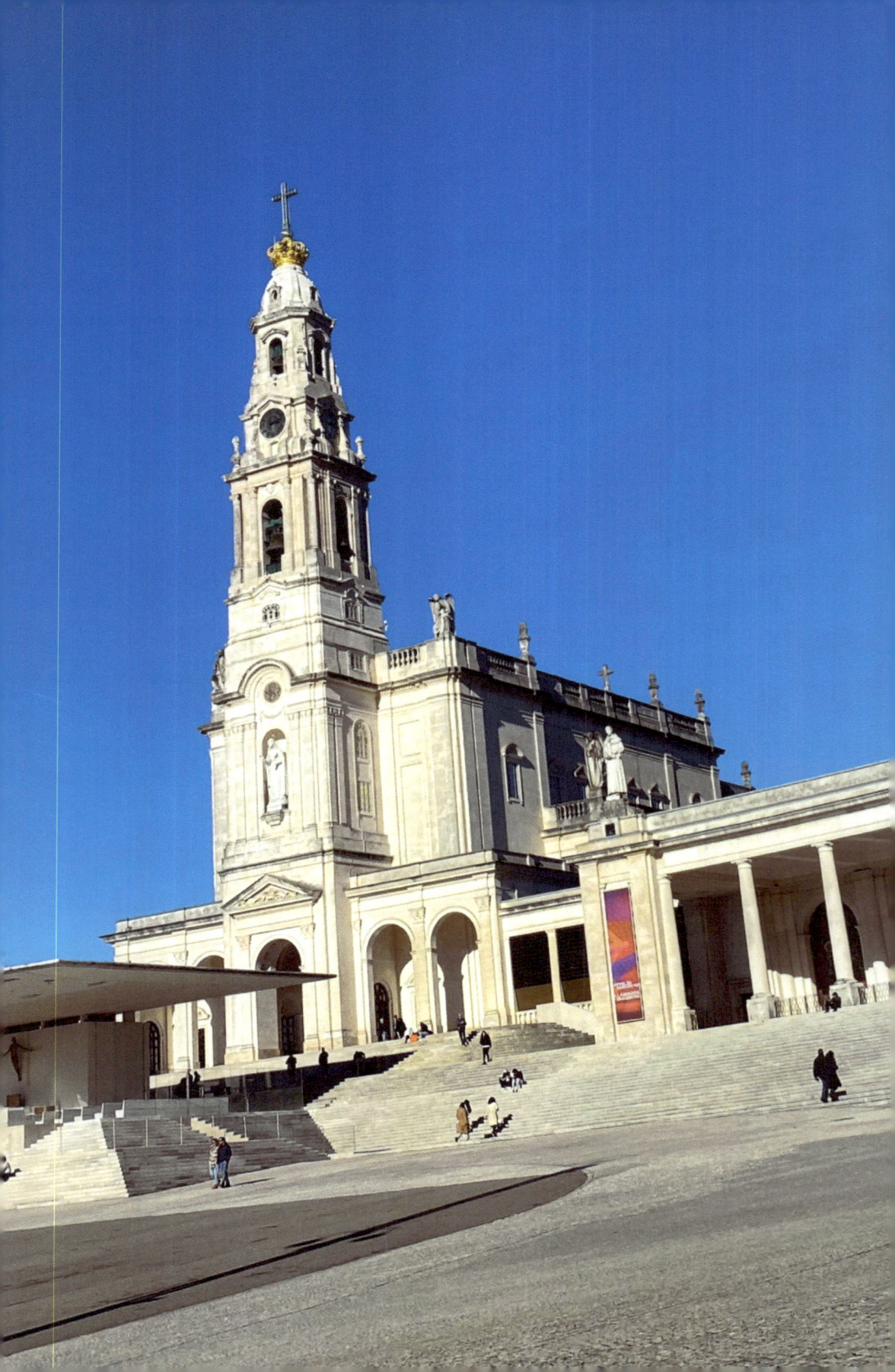

The Significance of the Rosary in Fatima:

Central to the Apparitions: During the six apparitions in 1917, the Virgin Mary repeatedly emphasized the importance of praying the Rosary daily for peace in the world and for the conversion of sinners. The Rosarium honors this message as a physical and spiritual space dedicated to prayer and reflection.

Symbol of Devotion: The Rosarium underscores the Rosary's role as a powerful spiritual practice, aligning with the Virgin Mary's call to "pray the Rosary every day.

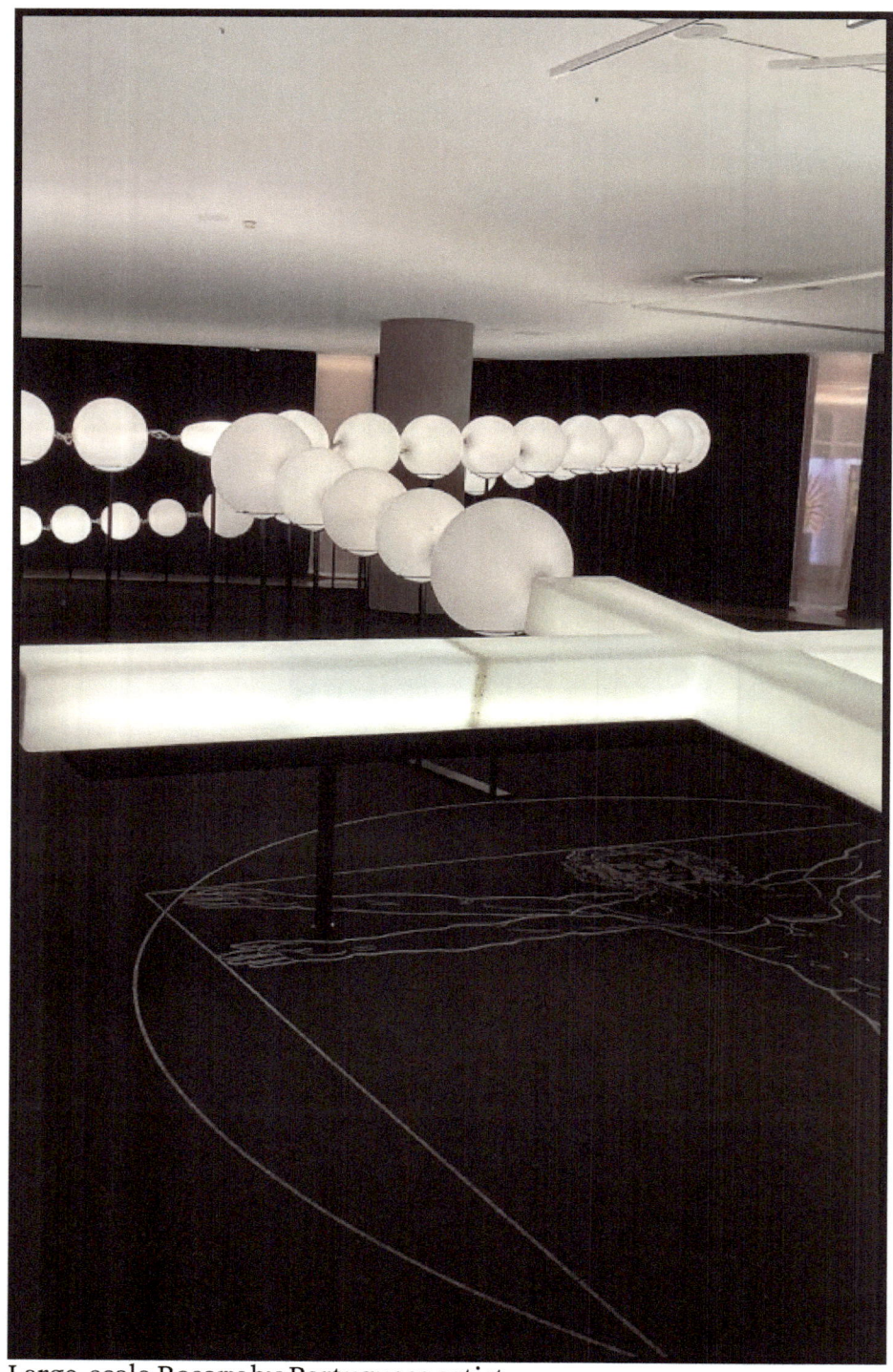

Large-scale Rosary by Portuguese artist Joana Vasconcelos - Rosarium - January 2024

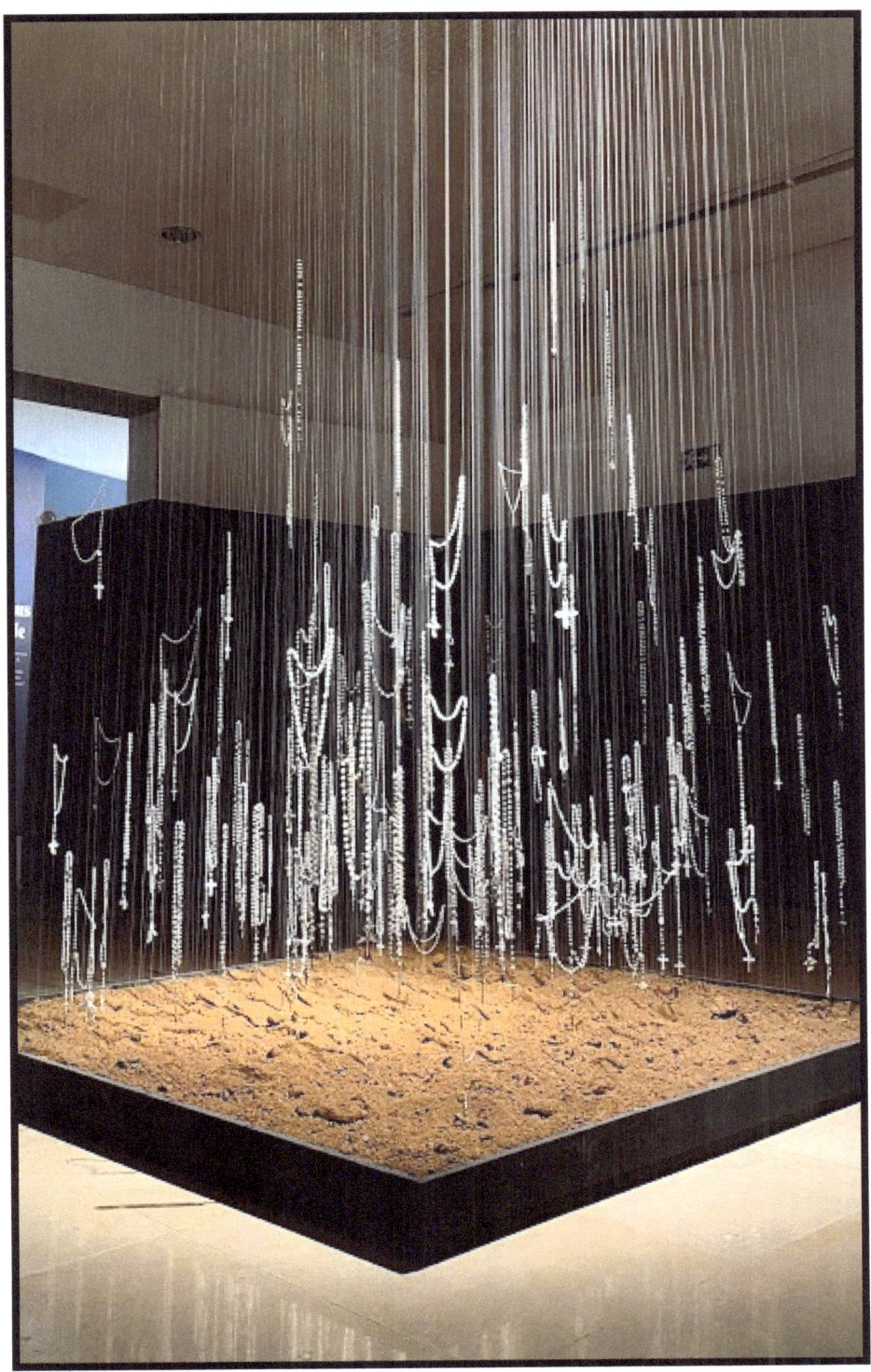

Rosarium - January 2024

The Rosary Museum in Fatima, often referred to as the Museum of the Shrine of Fatima, serves as a repository of historical, artistic, and religious artifacts tied to the story of the Marian apparitions and the site's significance as a global pilgrimage destination. Established to preserve the legacy of the Fatima apparitions, the museum offers visitors insights into the spiritual and cultural history of the region.

The museum houses a diverse range of artifacts, including textiles, sculptures, and objects that document the history of international pilgrimages and the daily life of the Fatima community during the 20th century.

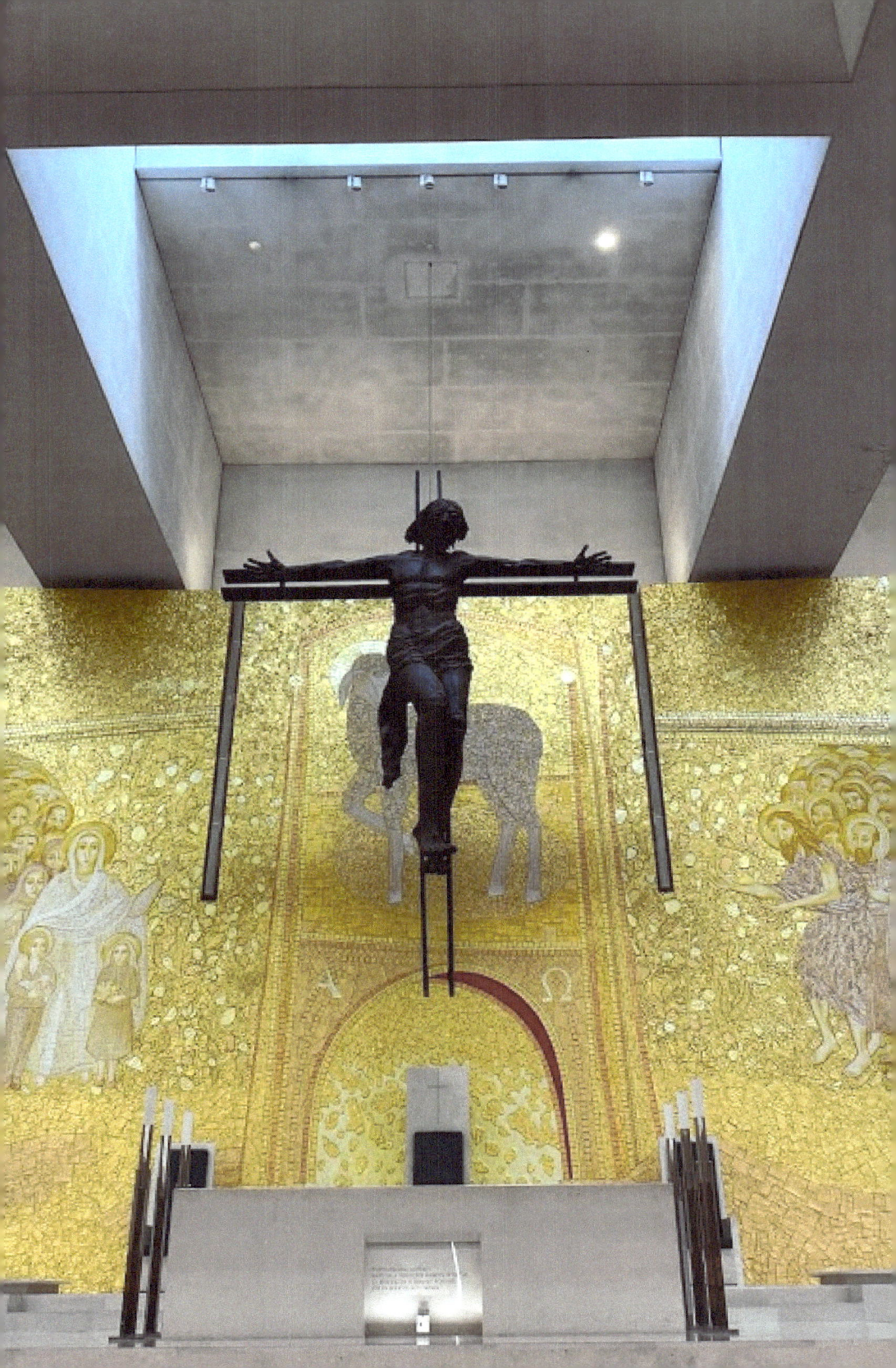

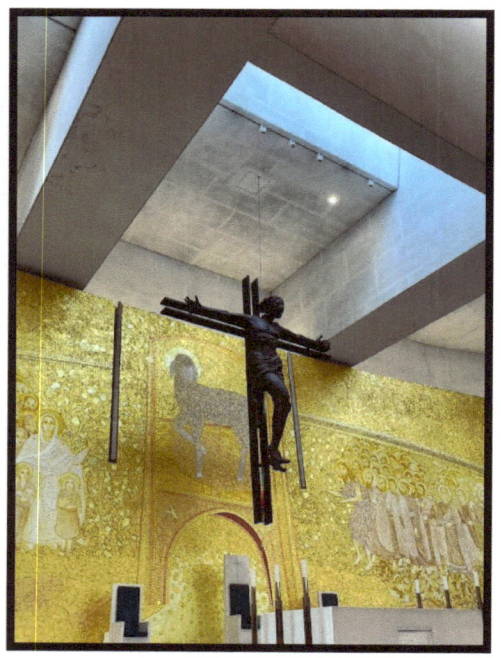
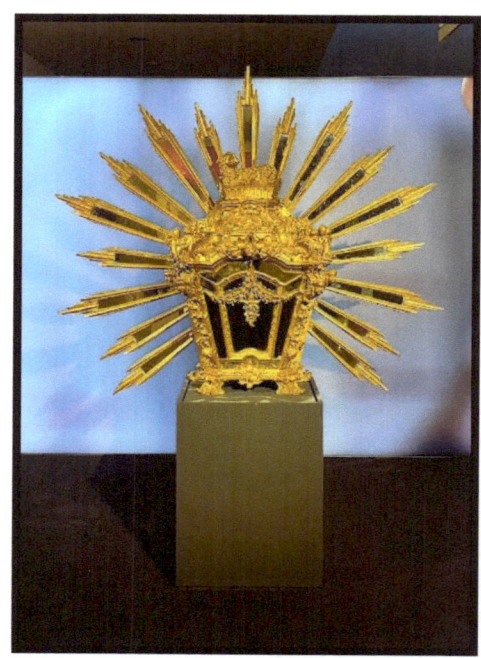
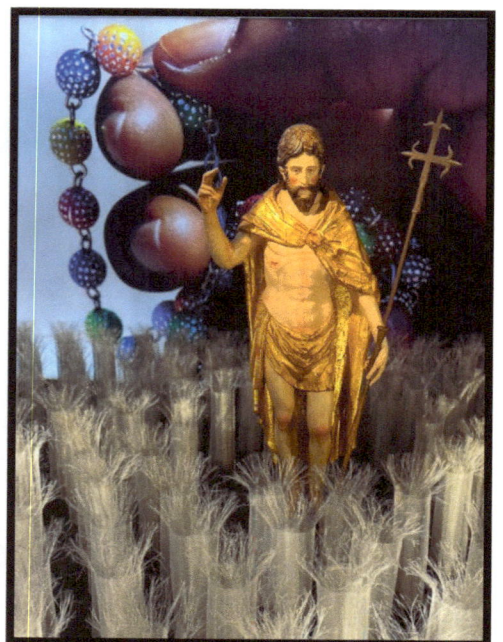
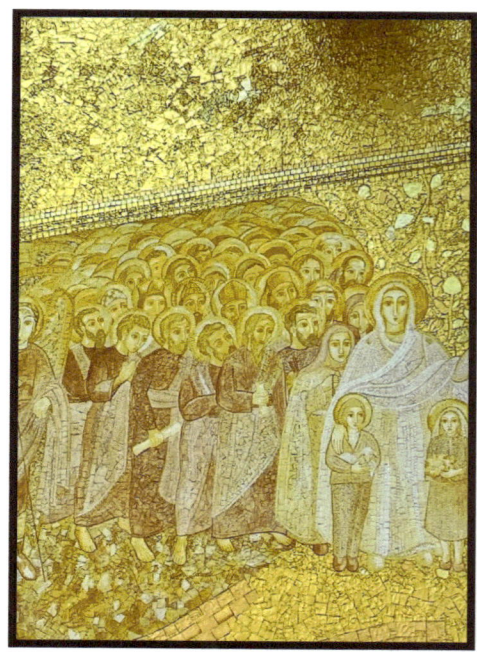

Shots from inside the Churh of the Holy Trinity and the Rosarium

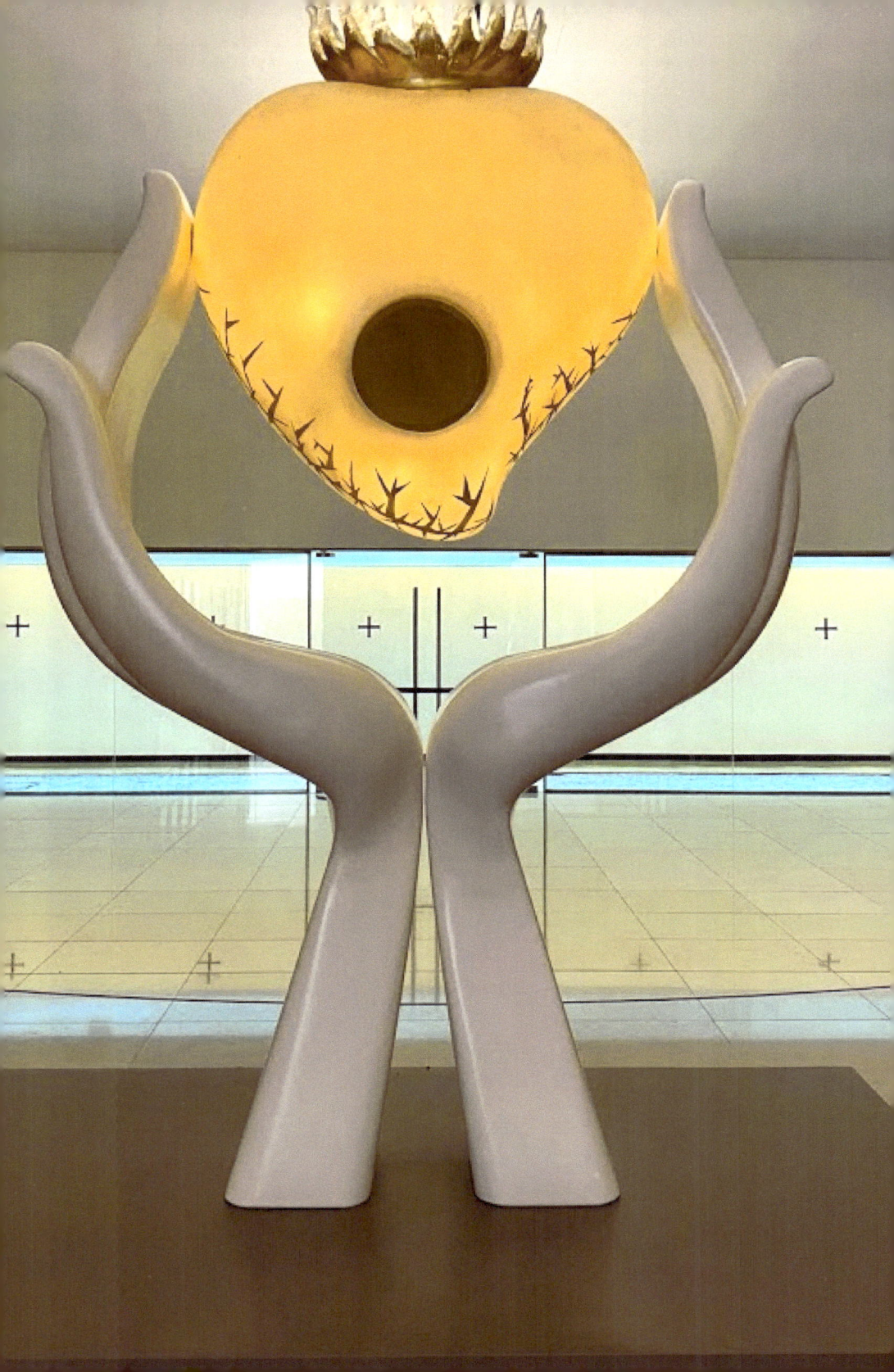

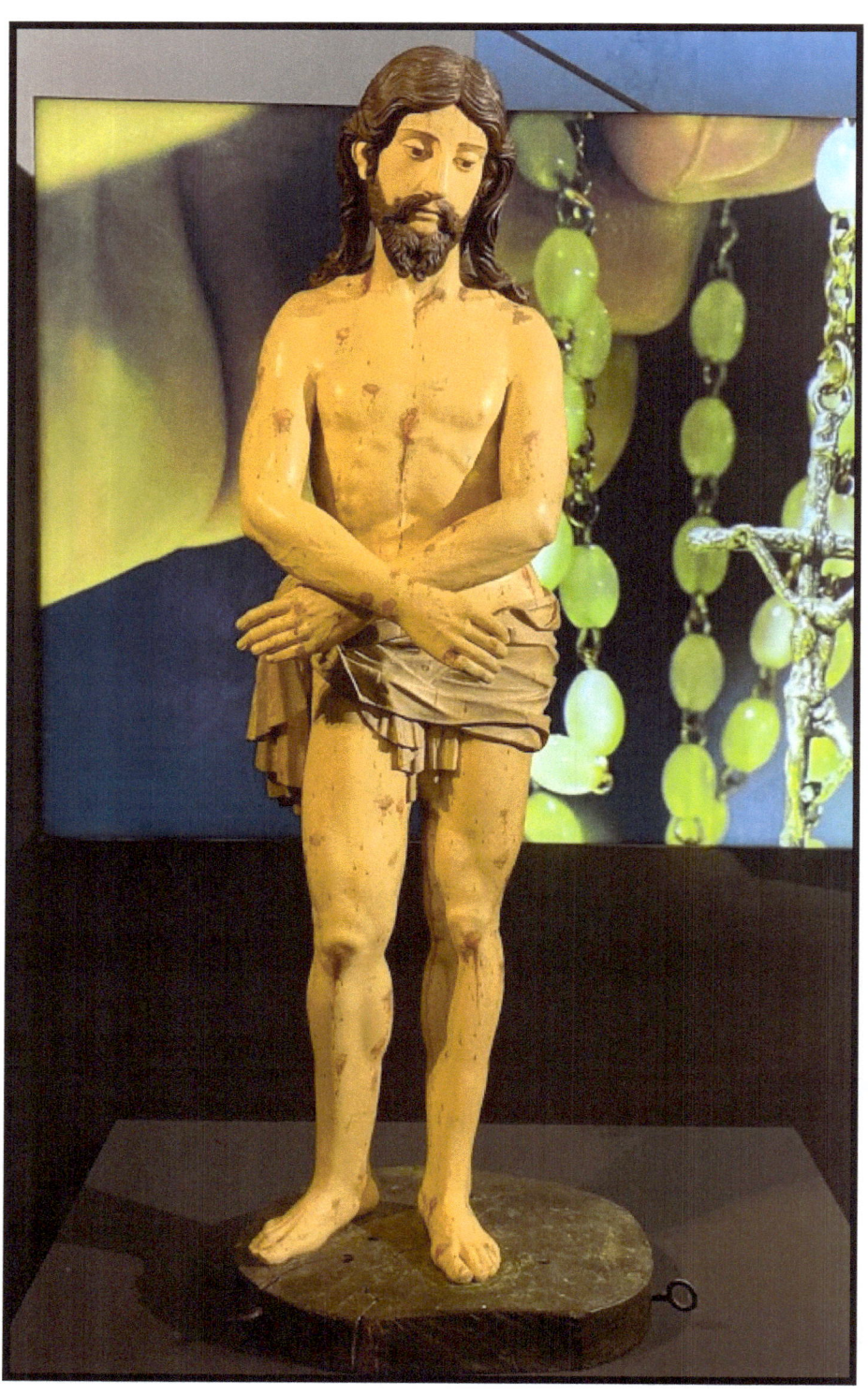

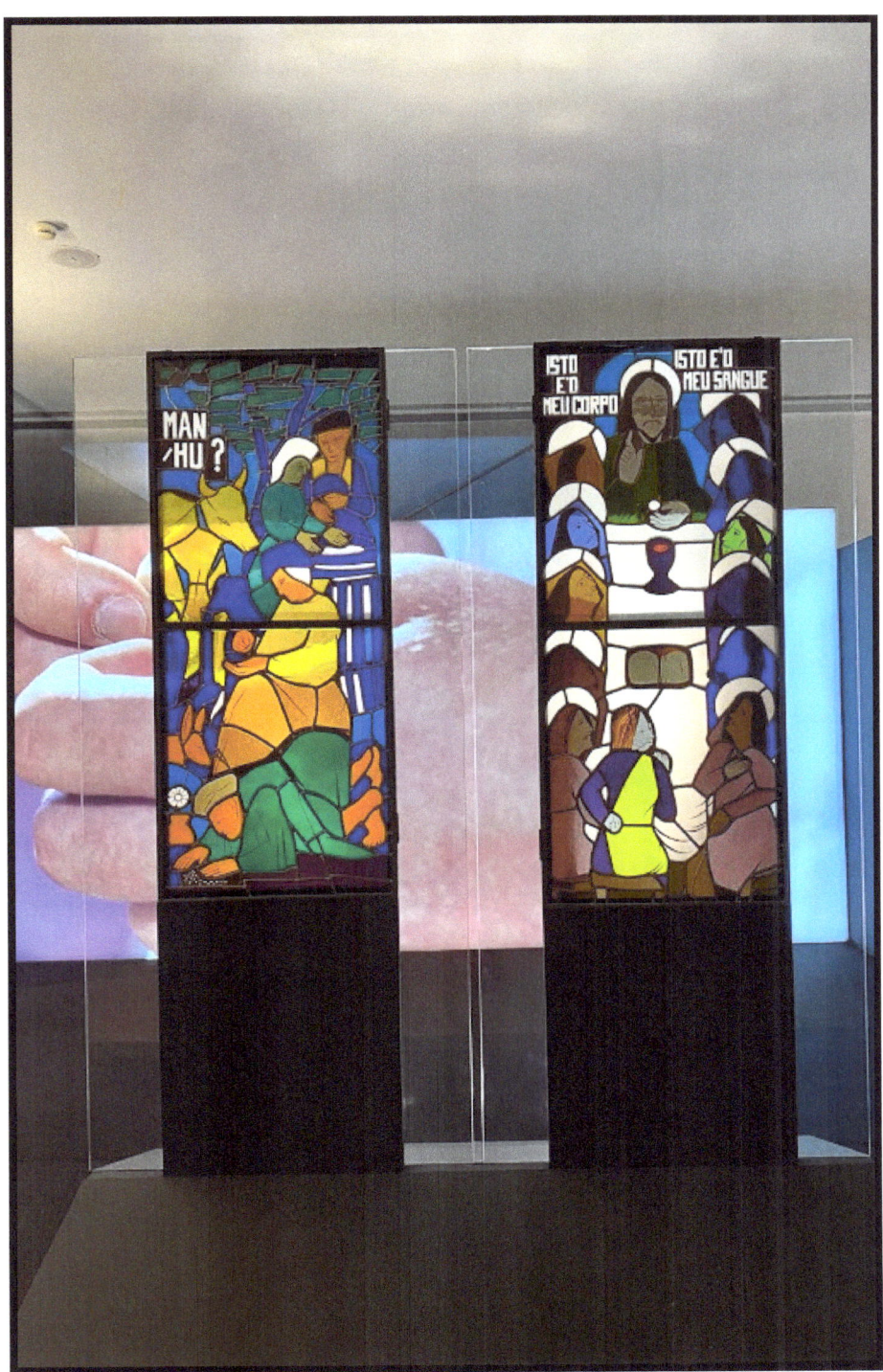

Rosarium - January 2024

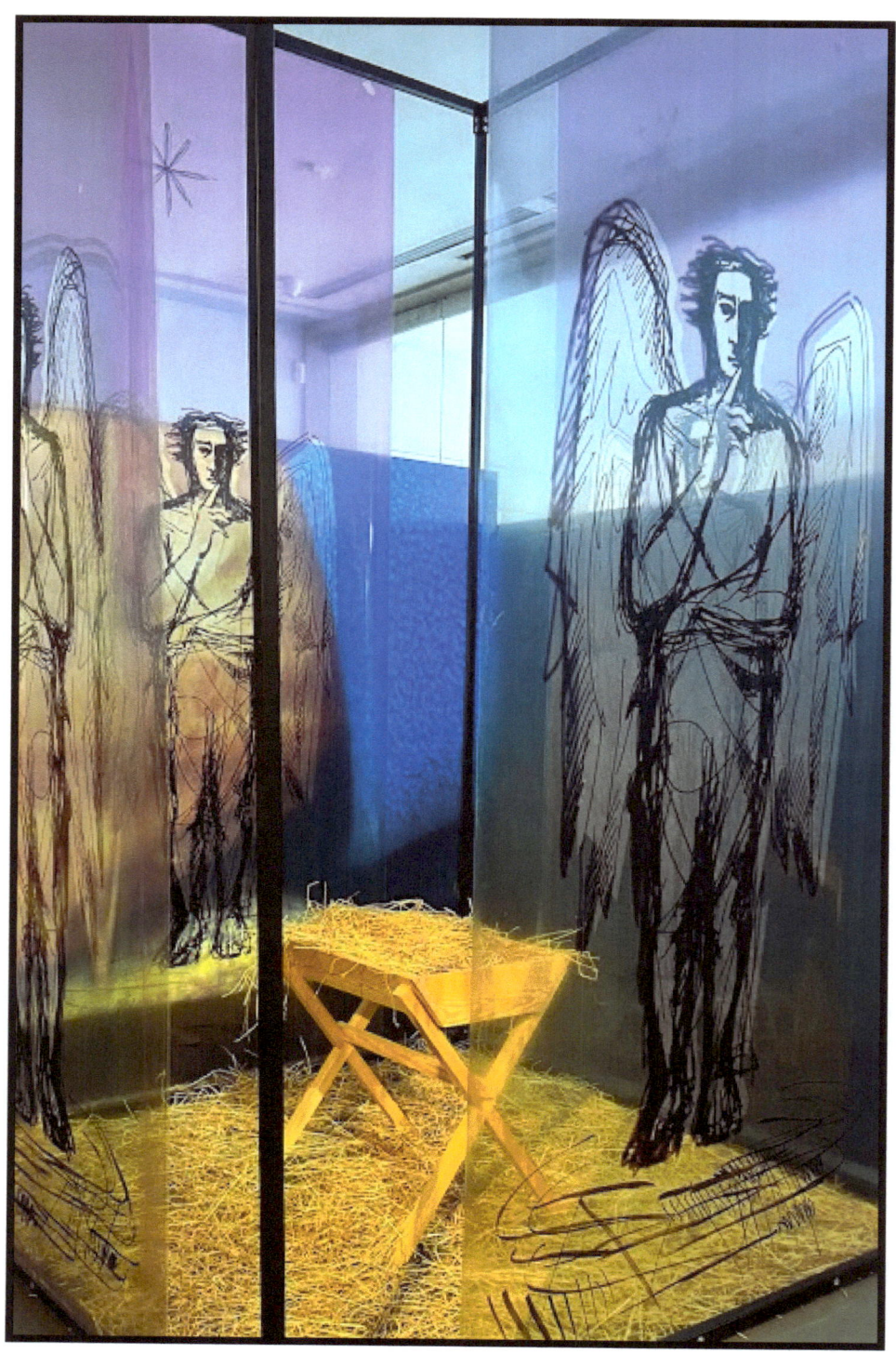

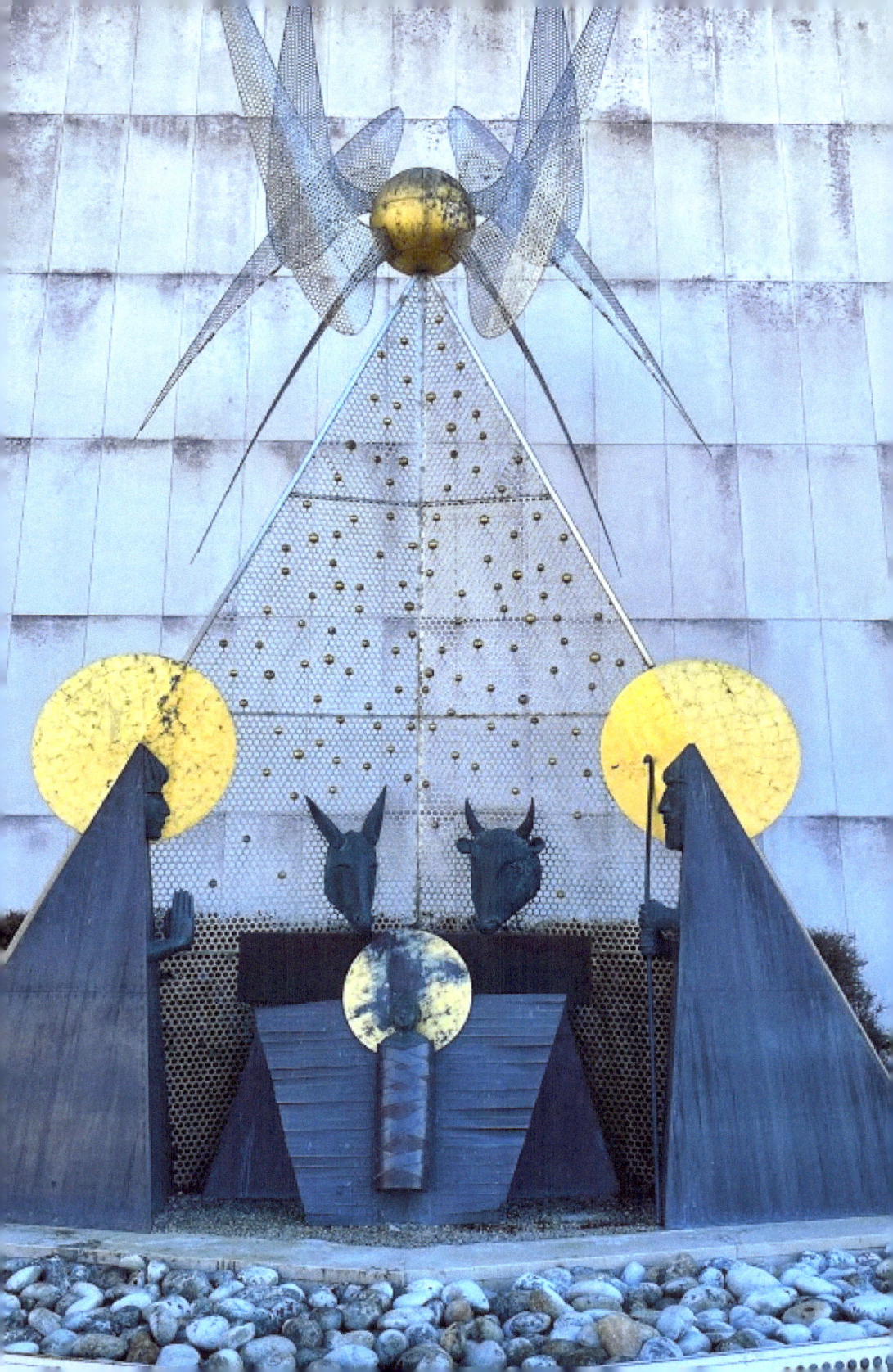

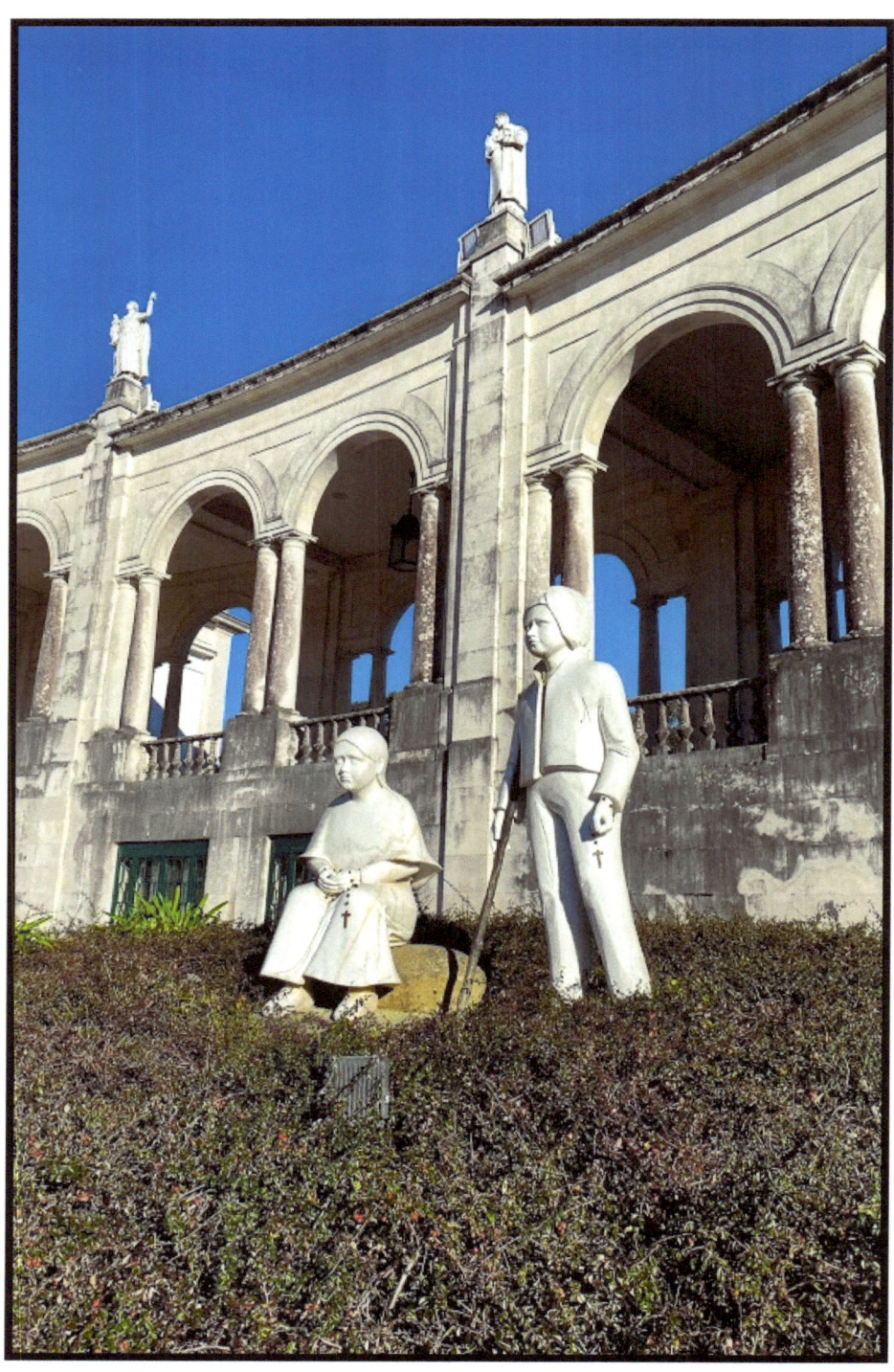

Statues of St. Francisco and St. Jacinta, the young shepherds who were present at the apparitions of Virgin Mary

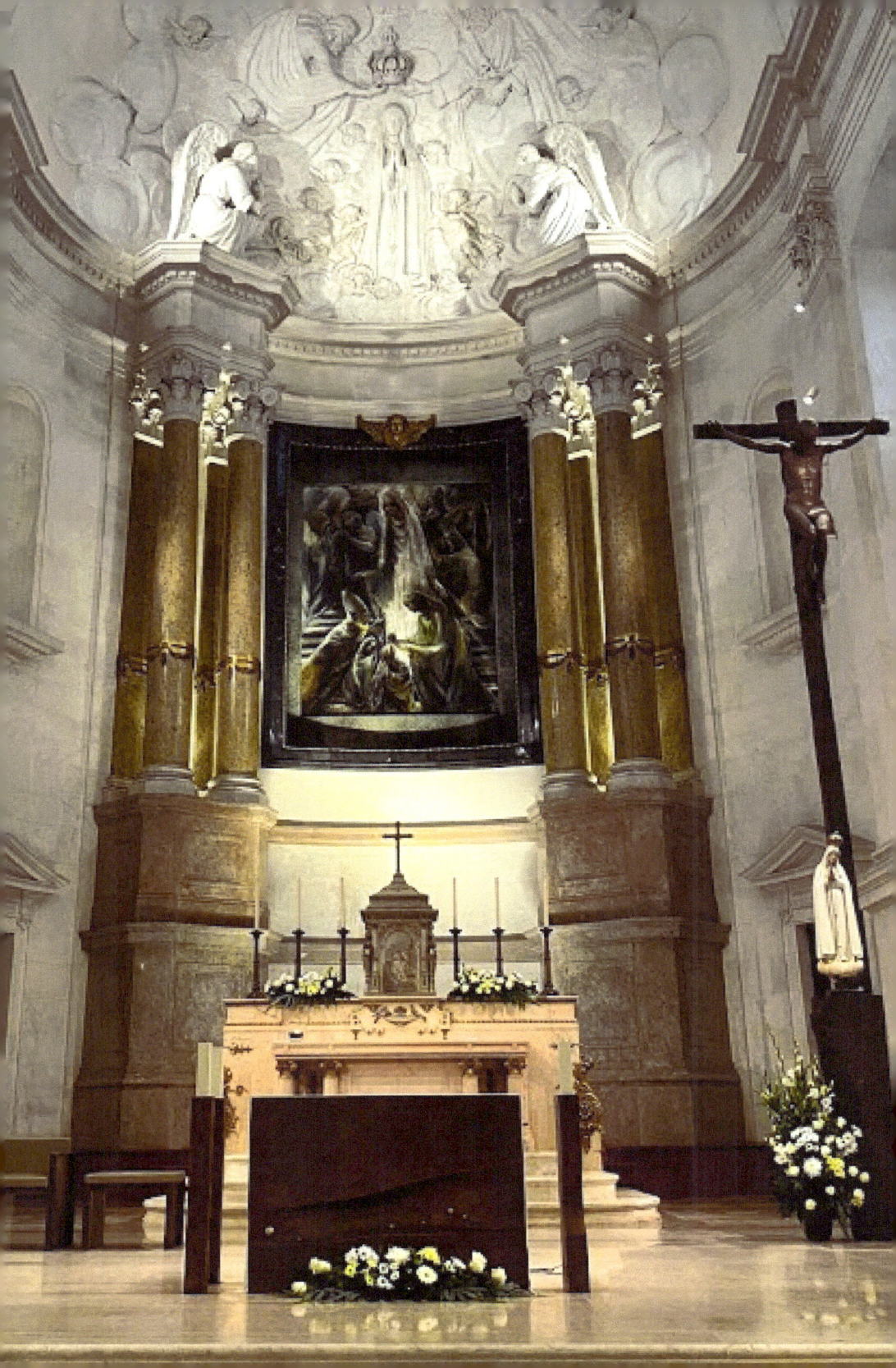

Architectural Details

The Basilica of Our Lady of the Rosary stands as a masterpiece of Neoclassical design, with its slender bell tower rising gracefully into the sky. Inside, the serene space holds the tombs of the shepherd children, marked by simple yet profound memorials. Nearby, the modern Basilica of the Holy Trinity provides a striking contrast, with its minimalist architecture symbolizing a forward-looking faith while honoring Fatima's timeless message.

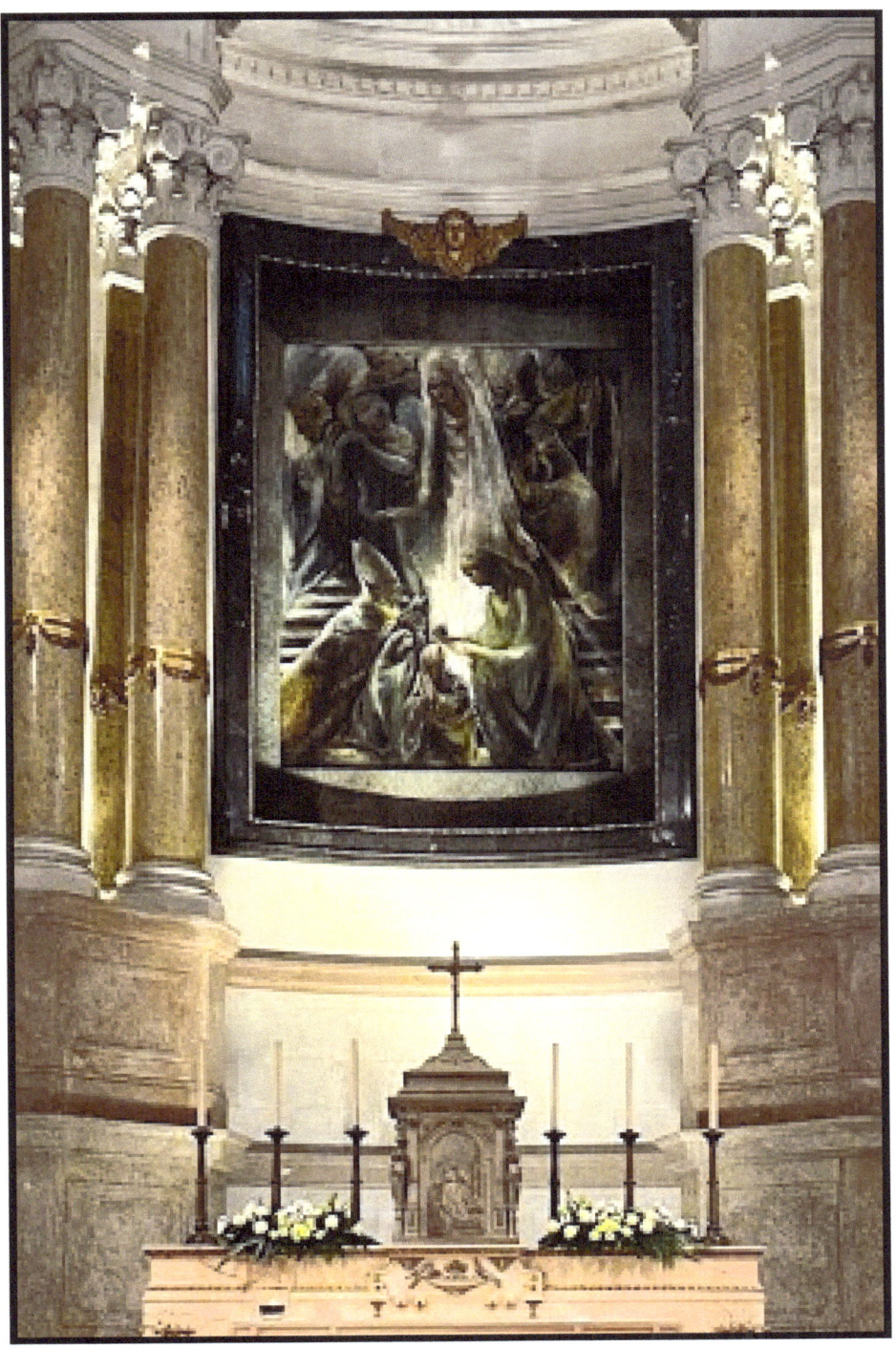

Main Altar inside the Sanctuary

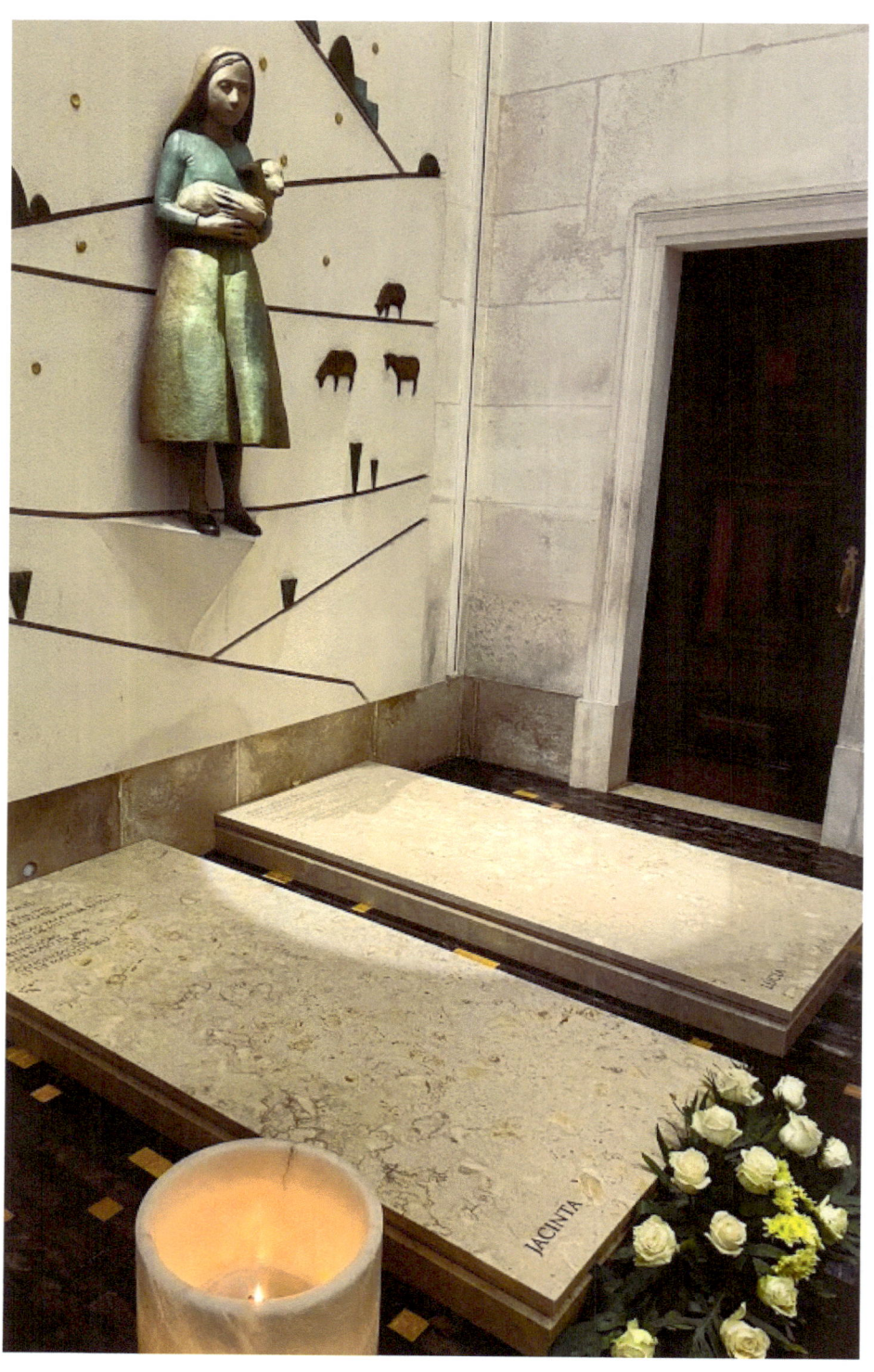

Tombs of the little shepherds Lucia and Jacinta - inside the Sanctuary

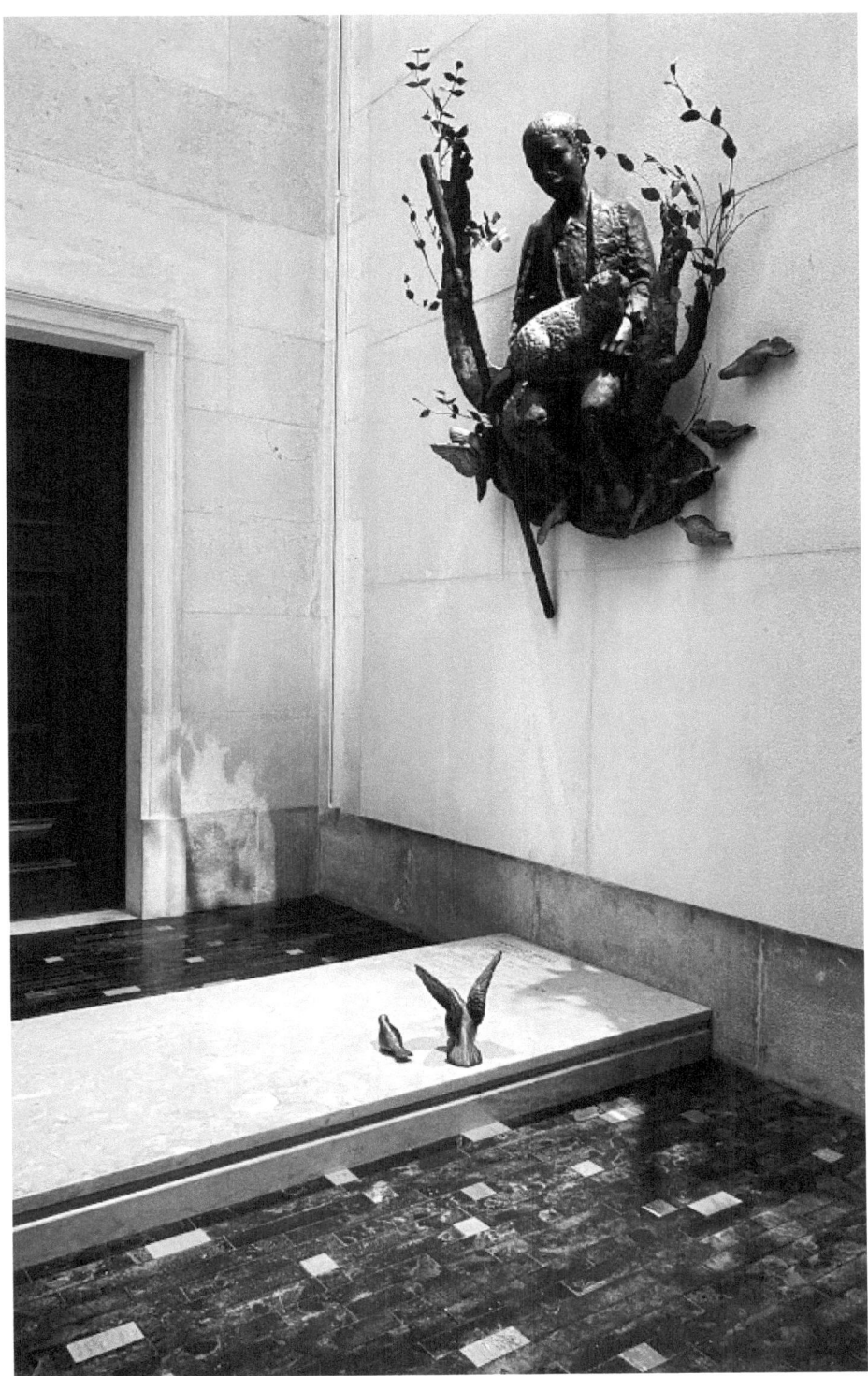
Tomb of the little shepherd Francisco - inside the Sanctuary

Lucia, Jacinta, and Francisco were ordinary children leading simple lives until their extraordinary encounters changed them forever. Francisco was known for his quiet devotion, often retreating to pray alone, while Jacinta displayed a compassionate spirit, offering sacrifices for others. Lucia, the eldest, became the voice of their experiences, dedicating her life to spreading Mary's message.

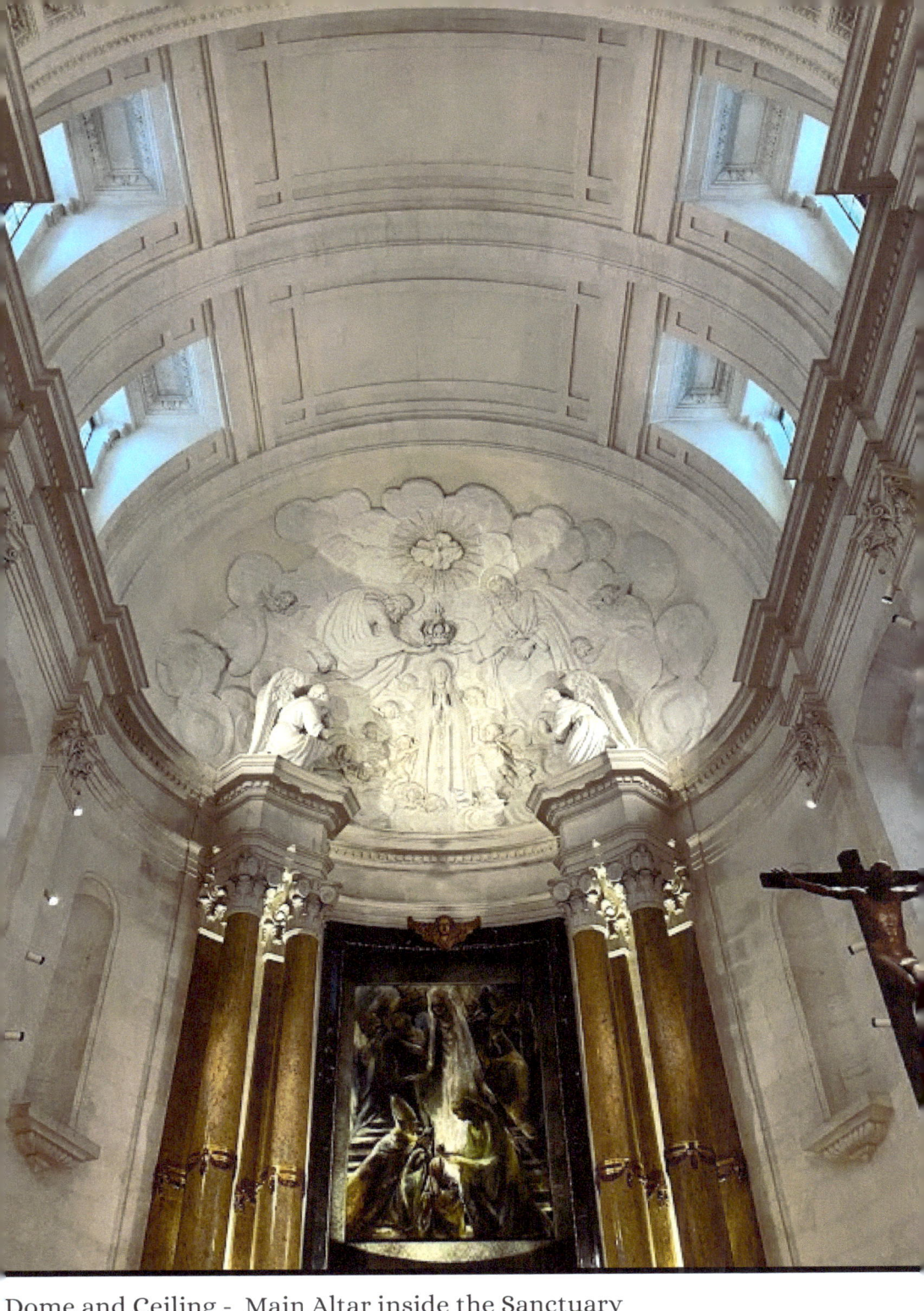

Dome and Ceiling - Main Altar inside the Sanctuary

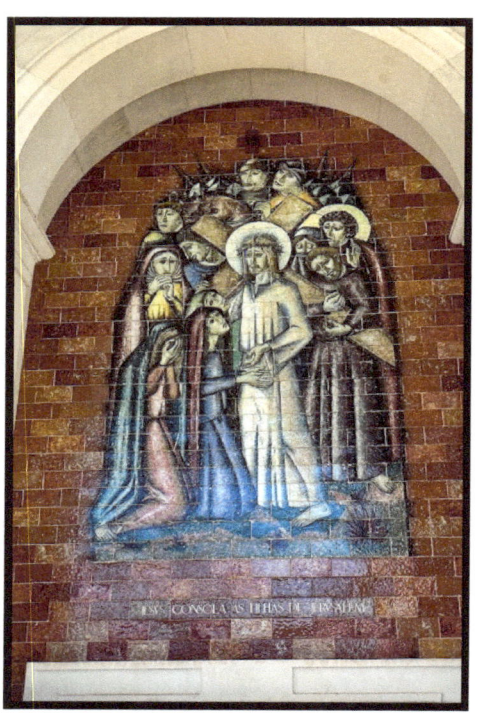
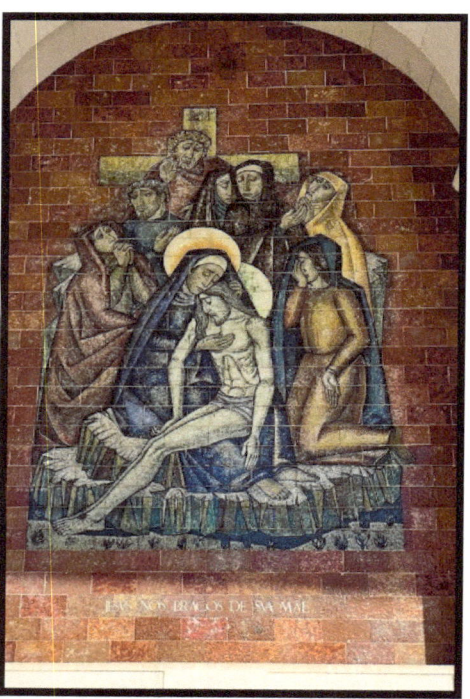

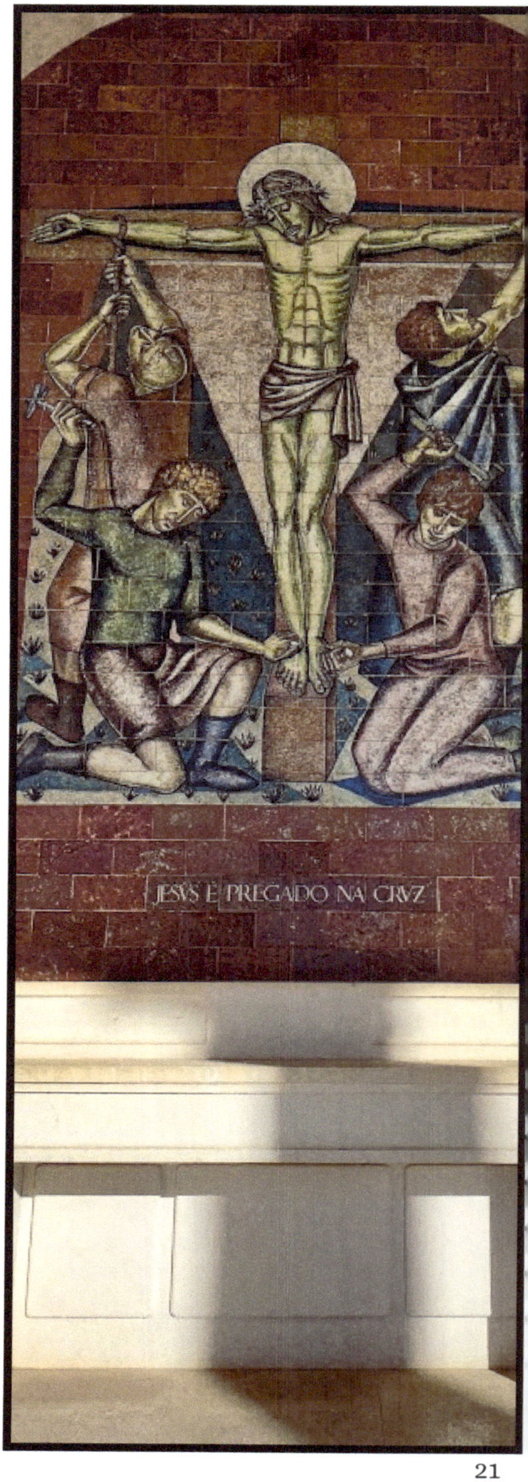

Depictions of the Passion of Christ

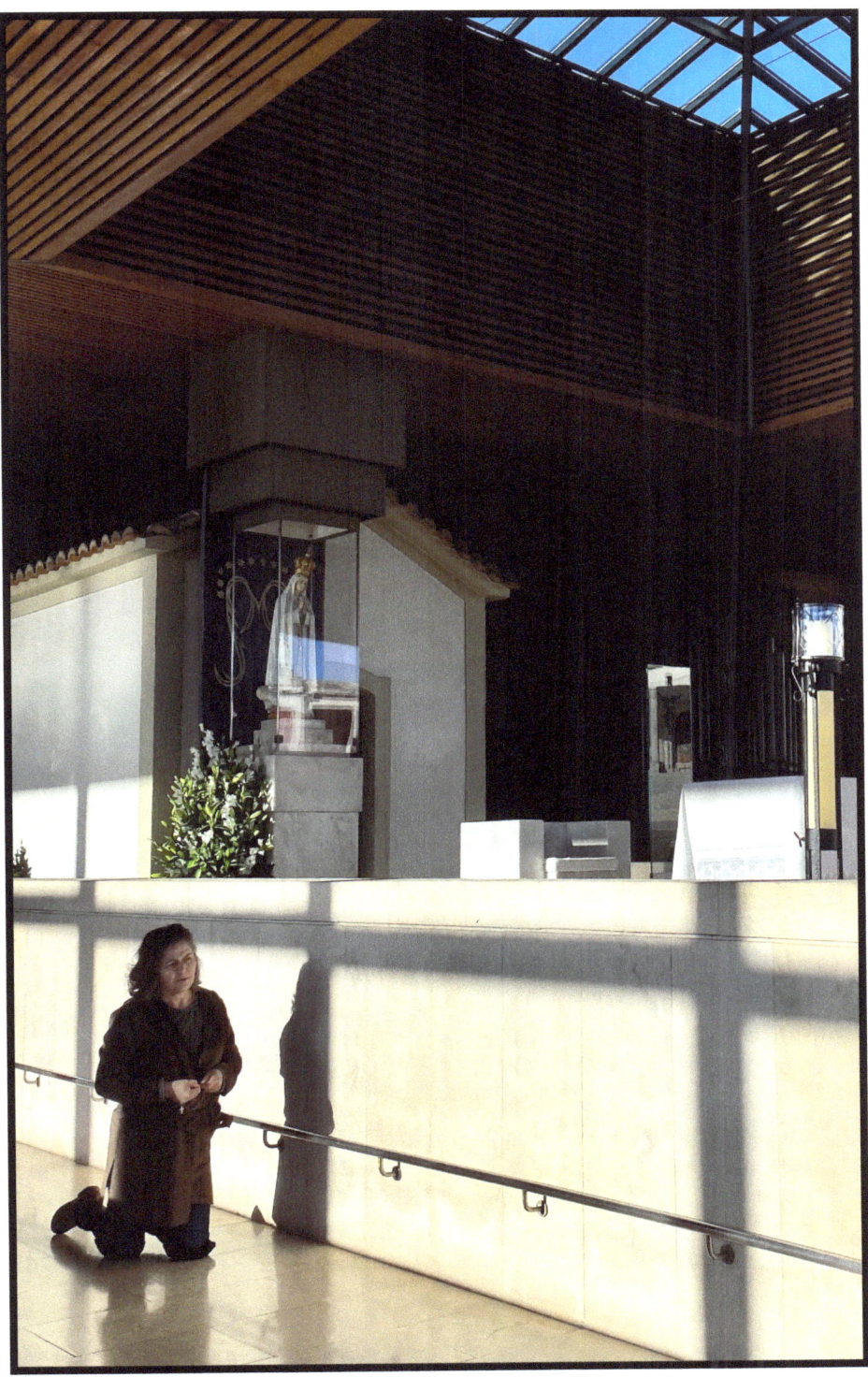

The Chapel of the Apparitions

Pilgrims arrive at Fatima from all corners of the globe, many walking for days to reach this sacred destination. Along the esplanade, you can see people kneeling and making their way to the Chapel of the Apparitions as a gesture of devotion and penance. Others light candles or write prayers, leaving them as offerings of faith and hope.

As you walk through the sanctuary, an overwhelming sense of peace envelops you. The gentle hum of prayers, the soft rustle of leaves, and the flicker of candles create a sacred ambiance that words can scarcely capture. Fatima feels like a bridge between the earthly and the divine—a space where time slows, and faith becomes tangible.

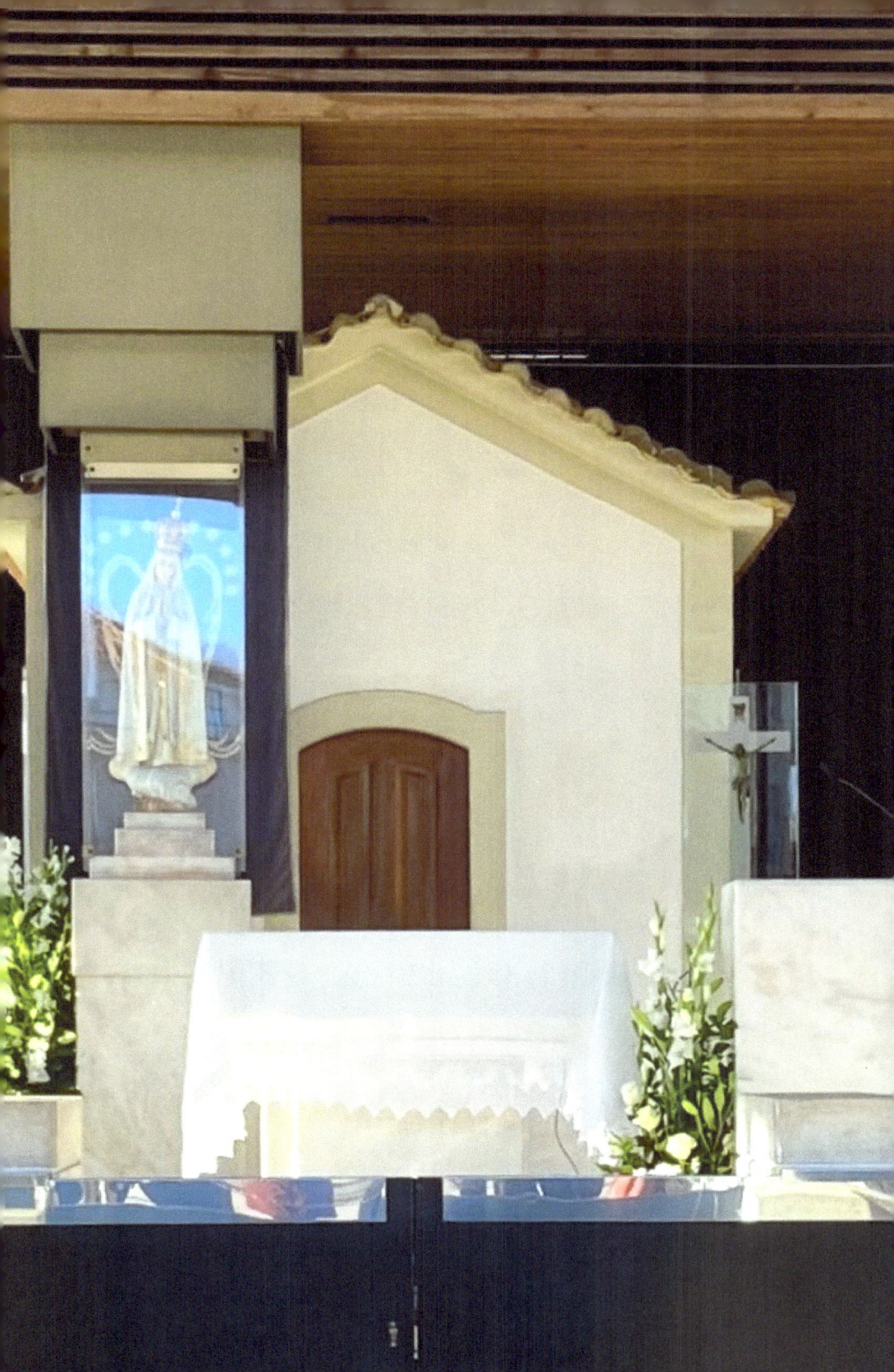

The Chapel of the Apparitions marks the exact spot where Our Lady first appeared. Its humble structure is a contrast to the grandeur of the surrounding buildings.

Nearby, the Valinhos is where Mary appeared after the children were briefly imprisoned, offering a poignant reminder of their steadfast courage and faith."

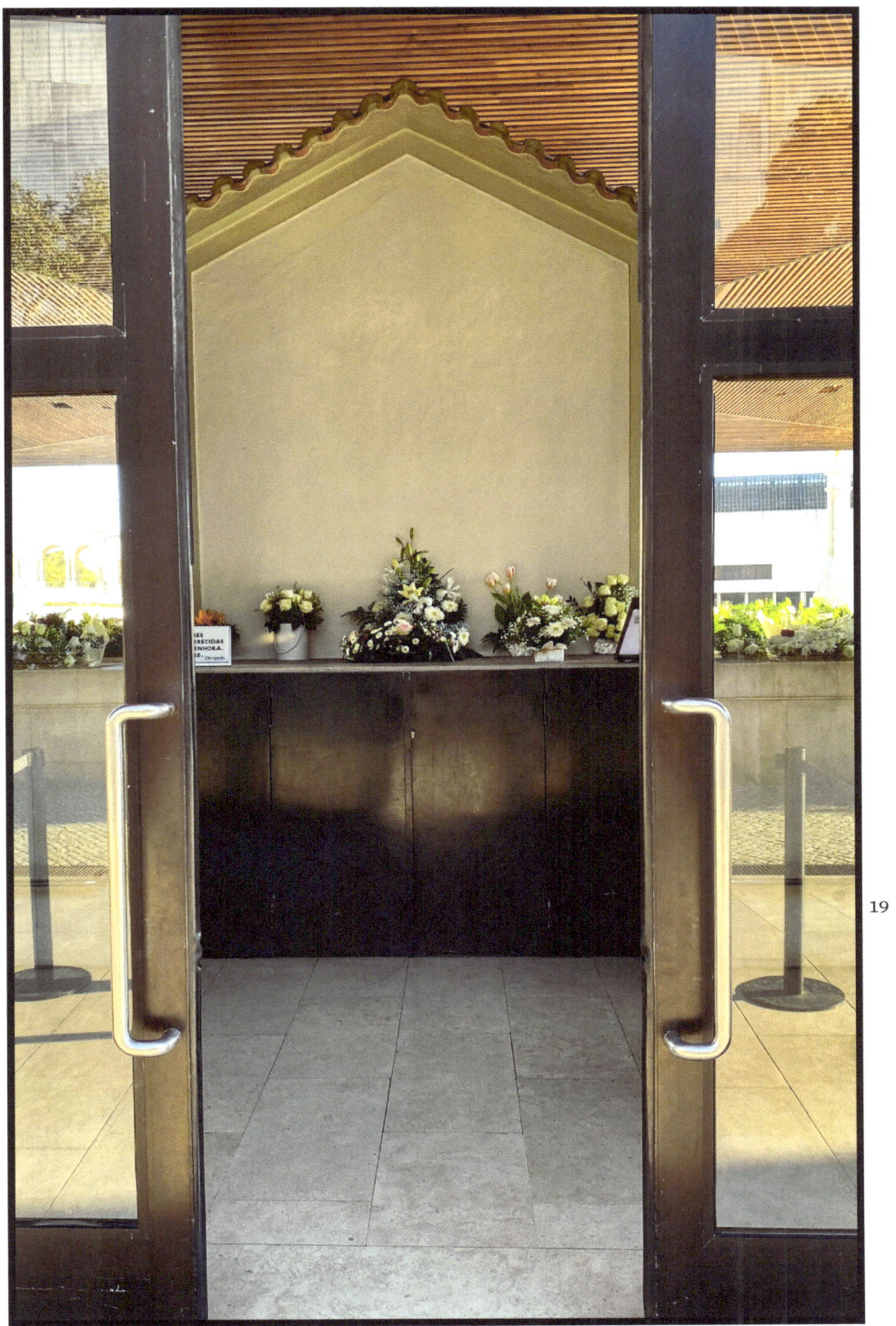

Back view of the Chapel of the Apparitions

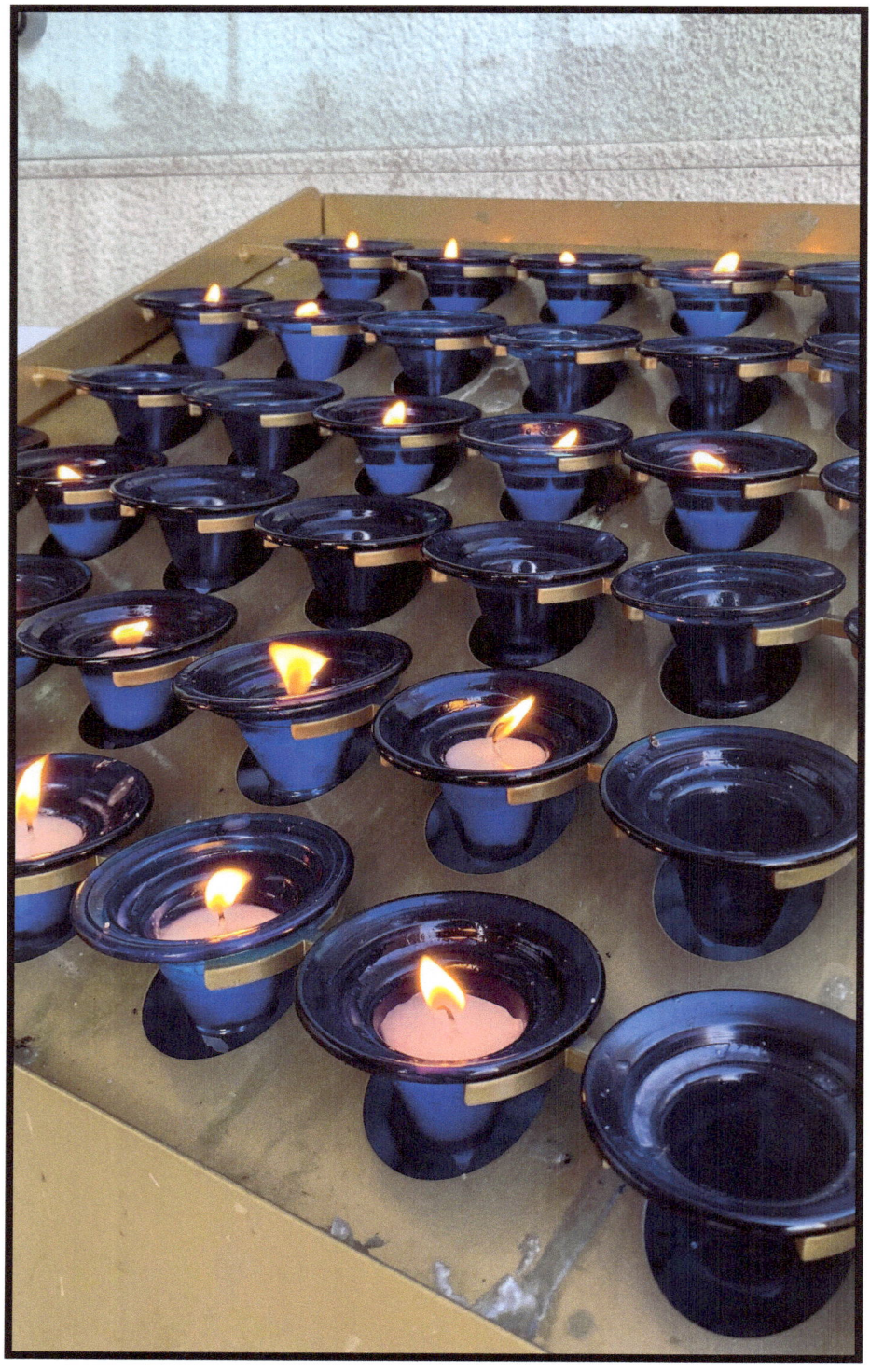

The miracles associated with Fatima, Portugal, are profound and central to its significance as a pilgrimage site. Here are some of the key miracles:

- **The Miracle of the Sun** (October 13, 1917): This is the most famous event at Fatima, witnessed by approximately 70,000 people. The sun appeared to dance in the sky, radiating multi-colored lights and seemingly plummeting toward the Earth before returning to its normal position. Observers described being able to look directly at the sun without discomfort, and many reported dramatic atmospheric changes during the event. The phenomenon coincided with the final Marian apparition to three shepherd children, Lucia, Francisco, and Jacinta, affirming their vision and messages from the Virgin Mary. The event has been extensively documented and remains a cornerstone of Fatima's spiritual narrative

- **Healing Miracles:** Pilgrims to Fatima have reported numerous healings attributed to prayers and intercessions to Our Lady of Fatima. Many faithful visit the Shrine to seek spiritual and physical renewal, and some have claimed miraculous recoveries from severe illnesses. While these are personal experiences rather than publicly verified miracles, they contribute to Fatima's reputation as a place of grace

- **Papal Protection**: Pope John Paul II attributed his survival of the 1981 assassination attempt to the intercession of Our Lady of Fatima. The bullet that struck him was later placed in the crown of the statue of the Virgin Mary at Fatima. This miraculous association deepened the shrine's global significance

Fatima's miracles continue to inspire faith and devotion, drawing millions annually to reflect on its spiritual messages of prayer, penance, and conversion.

www.ingramcontent.com/pod-product-compliance
Lightning Source LLC
Chambersburg PA
CBHW040259220526
45473CB00002B/528